To Denver with Love, Chiquita

Chiquita
Abbott
Farrell

Dayton Publishing

ISBN: 978-1-7351716-5-4

Title type: KG Love Somebody by Kimberly Geswein

Printed and bound on demand in the USA
to reduce waste in manufacture and delivery.

Dayton Publishing LLC
Solana Beach, CA 92075
858-775-3629
publisher@daytonpublishing.com
www.daytonpublishing.com

Linnea Dayton

To Nick —

*inventor, broker, Coast Guard veteran, boat captain,
motorcycle racer, appraiser and senior credit officer,
who still finds all the time it takes
to be my righthand man.*

Thank you.

Acknowledgments

Writing a book is harder than I thought, but more rewarding than I could ever have imagined. None of this would have been possible without my 4-foot-10-inch dynamic widowed mother, who always presented her best side for me and my sister. She set the course toward leadership and the skills that have made me the person I am today.

Much of this book was adapted from an interview conducted by oral historian Dr. Suzi Resnik and long-time Del Mar resident Don Terwilliger, originally recorded in 2011, and I thank them for that. The oral history was transcribed and added to over the years. In addition, I want to thank Larry Brooks and Martha Brooks for their keen insight, editorial help, and ongoing support in bringing my story to life.

I especially want to thank all the behind-the-scenes individuals who helped make this happen, and those who are the essence of this book and who truly make the story come alive.

Contents

Preface

As I come to the close of this cycle of experiences for me, this day begins with a question, "What about me, Chiquita Irene Cooper Abbott Farrell? What am I really about?" And what I learned from the man named Abbott was this: Every person is the sum total of every experience he or she has ever had, every one.

This is the story of the elder daughter of two young parents, who had made their move to California into another small town about the size of Del Mar. The daughter's name was Chiquita Irene Cooper.

I am that daughter, with her dad's mother and grandmother living next door. What a lucky start for me, because this must have helped me learn about the importance of family. Even to be able to experience "dress-up," sleeping overnight with Grandma Rosie and Great Grandma Marshy (Margaret), where both my sister Dona and I always received a chocolate while we were in bed listening to *Inner Sanctum* on the radio.

Then there were the dancing classes and performing, with family and others being in the audience. Whoopee! Receiving a huge bouquet of dahlias grown with pride by Grandma Rosie made the experience a real family affair. Fortunately, Grandma's lot next door included land enough to learn and practice baseball, so a few years later we could play ball with the boys and be able to brag about it. I remember, too, the old gnarly mulberry tree that was our own little spot where we could dream and pretend. Everyone needs such a private spot for reflecting.

I learned how to sew on a treadle sewing machine. I watched the ladies sew together quilts, even watched and finally experienced the tedious but satisfying job of moving a tiny sharp needle, pushing it into and through the fabric with the goal being an art piece. We girls really did not think of it as tedious. How happy everyone was when we were able to present a finished quilt with pride, showing it off to others. (The side benefit was that we could use it as a bed cover as well.)

I guess all this goes under the heading of learning that if you work hard enough to receive a warm welcome by others, then whatever endeavor you are involved with leaves a smile of pride on your face most of the time. Plus the importance of having your own private spot for reflecting.

Del Mar was off to a great start by the time our family arrived here. And then there appeared on the horizon some wonderful individuals and organizations that have contributed, and continue to contribute, to the life and character of Del Mar, some whose outsize influence has been notable. I'll take just a few pages in this book to acknowledge them and how they helped make Del Mar what it is today.

Were I to include all whom I've admired and who became my friends over the years, it would take many more pages, and to those not appearing here I apologize. Also, forgive my sharing some of my business transactions here. But frankly, I found them fascinating, and I hope you will also. I was lucky — so lucky, being able to put all these facts, negotiations and arrangements together over the years, at one of the finest West Coast beaches, a great vacation spot for tourists and also a wonderful home to long-term residents.

Chapter 1

I'll start at the beginning...

In 1924 I was born, thank goodness, and that was wonderful for me. My early years were in a small town very much like Del Mar. It was Monrovia, California, near Arcadia, in southeastern Los Angeles County. Everything in Monrovia was "down the street," very similar to Del Mar when I came here in the 1950s.

I was born of young parents, and three years later had one younger sister, Dona. Our Grandma Rosie (my dad's mother) and her mother, our great-grandmother, lived next door to us.

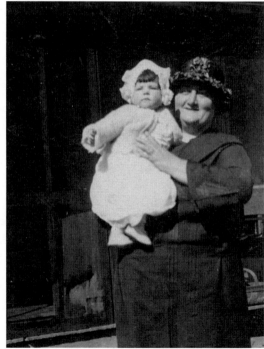

On the left, Daddy (Eldon Duard Cooper) and Mama (Vera Mae Rock Cooper); at right, Chiquita and Grandma Rosie (Rosa Lee Cooper) in 1925

As a little girl I attended dance studios and even performed at Saturday matinees during the Vaudeville era. That's what little girls did where we lived; there was so little other entertainment available to the theater

Chiquita, the Vaudeville days

Mama, Chiquita and Dona in January, 1933

operators. I recall that they even gave each adult attendee a piece of glassware, hoping they would keep coming often enough to collect a full set.

Our family experienced the 1933 earthquake. My sister and I were playing jacks in a corner of the living room, and the floor lamp swayed a lot and almost fell over. We ran outside, frightened. Our neighbors were having dinner in their dining room, and we could see their huge glass windows shake, but not shatter.

My elementary school was condemned because of quake damage, and as kids we felt we were lucky because we got to ride our bikes across town to a different school while ours was being repaired. I loved our "new" buildings when the repairs were done.

In grade school I came home for lunch, a daily race with myself for a better time than the day before. I was one of the few girls in our end of Monrovia; there were more boys than girls. The roads saw cars so seldom that we kids used to play in the street, this game called "kick the can." Can you picture that today — can you imagine?

Big changes in our young lives

The Navy had prepared my dad for early "tech." He wired the very first intercity telephone board for California Water & Telephone, serving the communities of Monrovia, Arcadia and Duarte. Somewhere I have a photo that shows the actual wired telephone board to be something like 8 feet by 24 feet, not much larger than one of my living room walls. It is really very interesting to think about it in comparison to communication today. Now, almost 100 years later, we have today's smart phones — Android, iPhone — and an abundance of other devices.

Well, we lost our dad to a heart attack when I was 10 and he was just 36, so my tiny mother (really only about 4 feet 10 inches tall), was left with two little girls to look after. She had a third-grade education, and she had never been employed nor paid any of the usual household bills.

Aren't grandmothers really wonderful? Besides contributing money to our family's support, my grandmother provided special things and extra fun. Grandma Rosie used to walk my sister and me to the Saturday movie with a dime hidden under each of her leather gloves, one for each of us to retrieve and spend on ice cream.

The circle of life continues...

While in grade school, I had a couple of really memorable teachers. One was Mrs. Kolb. Now, remember the days of Cutex nail polish? Mrs. Kolb changed the color of her nails with each outfit, and this was very impressive to a third-grader.

A few years ago while I was sitting in Jake's Del Mar resaurant at a Friends of the Powerhouse board meeting, I overheard Darrell Mueller say he was going to ride in a vintage Ford in the Monrovia Day Parade. What a surprise! I had been sure I was the only one in Del Mar who knew of Monrovia. The story becomes more interesting, for later Darrell and I figured out that his aunt, a teacher in Monrovia, was in fact my third-grade teacher, Mrs. Kolb!

That day at Jake's, Darrell suggested that Steve Farrell, long-time Del Martian and by then my husband of several years, and I go out to the parade. He even directed us to where we would have the best view, and we arranged to meet up with his group while we were there.

So Steve and I drove out, and we really did so enjoy being there and even saw two shops that were still there from when I was a youngster. We walked the couple of blocks to the Monrovia Library. I remembered the building so well — the many steps leading to the entrance, and the date stamp attached to the librarian's pencil, which she used each time I took out a book.

The library seemed so small to me now. Children's early impressions are remembered all their lives; things are grander in those memories.

The next event of the day was to try to locate the various houses I had lived in — what a patient man Steve Farrell was, and we did just that.

We walked down the alley in back of one house, and there was a young man who was working on his car. He asked our reason for "walking the alley," and I introduced myself.

"Oh, the Coopers," he said. He then invited us into his home (my grandmas had lived in the little house at the back of the lot next door, which his family now owned). In we went — and my goodness, everything looked the same! It was a Craftsman design, but all of the houses in the neighborhood were very small, just cottages. He then showed me the back porch, where we found my initials, and those of my sister and my mother as well. Now that was an experience!

By the end of our adventure, I was pretty excited, for I had also located the other two places we had occupied — rather untouched, even the double garage of the one we lived in at the time of the earthquake. And I remembered that our dad had installed a little phone with a wire that led from the two-story garage into the house. We had a total of two "instruments." True, the phones were very primitive by today's standards, but they worked … real excitement!

On to high school

My high school years (1938–1942) were spent in another community close to South Pasadena, where I lived with my other grandmother (Grandma Ma) and auntie because of the nearby high school/junior college, called L. A. Pacific College, which was affiliated with their evangelical church. This grandmother, my mother's mother, had become convinced I was being raised too loosely. Perhaps because of my Vaudeville appearances? Or kick the can?

Grandma Ma (Edith Hamilton), my maternal grandmother

Well, that began another period of learning and experiencing all that was deemed appropriate for young ladies from 14 through 18 attending a Christian school. We went to mid-day chapel at school, went to prayer meeting, and Sunday all day there were church activities. Fortunately, I was sent home to my mom and sister on some weekends. They had moved to South Pasadena so we could all live close together.

I remember when I was 17 and living in South Pasadena, I had just returned from church (located down the street from our apartment) when I heard on the radio that Pearl Harbor had been attacked. It must have been President Roosevelt who announced it, but all I remember is that it was big and serious news. Headlines all over!

Chiquita Cooper, at L. A. Pacific College

Unfortunately, I did not have the necessary background, or was not mature enough to know all the implications of this event. Did any of us? We did not have televisions, and daily newspaper delivery was hardly the norm. I can picture myself standing on the landing of a concrete stairway, because my boyfriend took my picture after church.

Perhaps it's good that youngsters are not always fully aware of what is happening outside their small environment! I have looked back to that time and recognized how much more the children of today are exposed to the great world around them — much more than we were.

In high school I believe we were studying how the starving children of China were surviving. And then there was Africa. The answer was missionaries I believe. When we were older, we were always taught Latin, Spanish and French, and if you were smart enough — and probably a religion major — Greek.

High school was important, for that is where I met Bill Abbott, the young man I would marry a few years later. We would soon have our two wonderful boys, and before long we would be a part of their childhood in Del Mar.

Bill Abbott and Chiquita Cooper, in their junior and freshman years respectively, at L. A. Pacific College in 1939

Chapter 2
Coming to Del Mar

I remember my first fall in Del Mar in 1956, when Bill Abbott, my husband and the boys' dad, had been hired for a newly created position: a consulting psychologist with the San Diego County schools. His job was to travel throughout San Diego County, to meet the teachers and begin to make them aware of the fragility of children's feelings about themselves and toward each other.

This new concept was not necessarily well received, for at that time one really never ever spoke of going to a psychologist for therapy, much less introducing it to the elementary schools. Later, when Bill and I attended local affairs such as PTA meetings or Chamber of Commerce activities (there was not much else going on socially), as we were about to be introduced to others I would whisper to him, "Do we know them?" His response was usually "No," although I knew he was working as a psychologist with a certain child on behalf of these parents. Later it was I who was acquainted with them from a real estate point of view, with another kind of very private access. Privacy issues were important during those times; that's the way it was. I am hopeful the same respect for privacy exists today in those professional relationships.

Did you know that in 1956 children in Bonsall, as well as in Julian, not so many miles from Del Mar, rode their horses back and forth to school? Before I came to Del Mar I had never heard of places where that happened, having come from such civilized environs as Pasadena, outside of Los Angeles.

Del Mar life
Living in the small beach community of Del Mar was a delightful change for us. In Pasadena I had been working as an executive secretary for the CEO of a very heavy industrial firm in downtown Los Angeles. Even at

that time, there was so much automobile traffic there — whew, what a relief it was to be here!

At the time, when we lived in our rental home on Coast Boulevard at the north end of Del Mar, I was able to carry my heavy-but-portable typewriter to the sand. I sat down and wrote home to my mother: "Guess where I am? Sitting on the beach just down from where we go to pick up our daily mail," and I typed on and on.

Well, there was this very tall man I often saw crossing the street in our neighborhood. He was dressed in short pants, barefooted and carrying a big coffee mug.

How intriguing…I thought people always had to go to an office to work — not stay home and wander the neighborhood. I wanted to know more. Later on, I learned that he called himself an *investor*. What was an investor? Walking around in the morning at home? I had no idea.

I learned more, and was I ever impressed! So my goal was to become "an investor in Del Mar." Wasn't that fun? He and his wife later invited me into their small cottage down the street, and there in their tiny living room was a huge computer. All of the stock market activity was there on the screen for him to follow while at home. Do remember, this was the fall of 1956. He and his wife were a part of this neighborhood that I later named "the Beach Colony."

During the school year, all of Del Mar was truly a sleepy place to live, because most of the small beach houses were owned by San Diego residents, who would drive up for weekends and summer vacations. I shall always remember my earliest impressions, for I had known nothing of this lifestyle before. It wasn't until nearly a year later that I learned that Del Mar's thoroughbred racetrack drew the cars and visitors that made it come alive during the summer, with excitement and more people.

A sense of the surroundings

When we first came to Del Mar, there was no I-5 freeway, so Highway 101 was the only north-south artery and the main road to San Diego. Our rental on Coast Boulevard on the north end of town was within a few feet of "the highway" as we called it. We were just down the street from Don Terwilliger's family home, where they lived in a house Don's mom and dad had bought in 1946 after living in five other houses in Del Mar before that one. Don was in Hollywood at the time they lived on Coast.

The El Adobe Motel was on the triangular southeast corner at 22nd Street and Coast. It's still there today as the El Adobe Apartments.

This aerial photo shows the Beach Colony neighborhood of Del Mar, south of the San Dieguito River, west of Highway 101, and north of about 18th Street. The El Adobe Motel (now El Adobe Apartments) is in the triangular lot formed just south of where Coast Boulevard and Highway 101 meet. Our rented duplex was just a little south of there. The inset photo has been retouched to represent the area as it was when we lived there in the 1950s, with more unbuilt lots than when the more extensive photo was taken in 1988.

A postcard from the El Adobe Motel

To the rescue!

And, of course, there were many gas stations on Highway 101 in Del Mar then; some people called this part of the highway "Gasoline Alley." But oh, the highway and its reputation! By the time they had battled the two-lane Highway 101 from L. A. to Del Mar, drivers were tired or intoxicated. As they headed up the hill into town in a hurry, with Coast Boulevard 40 to 50 feet below to the west, they sometimes failed to notice the slight curve in the highway until it was too late, and they drove off the edge of the road and down the embankment behind our little place on Coast near 22nd Street. We were there for accident after accident.

We had a little routine for "assistance." I would go to the phone to call the fire department, the boys would be told to stay inside the fence, my husband Bill would get a shovel, and then he and I would be ready to run to help, or at least observe.

I remember one night a car flipped over as it went off the road and down the embankment. So Bill ran with his shovel (across three vacant lots between our house and the bottom of the embankment), and our rescue proceedings were in play. Please picture this: Wanting to prevent the engine from catching on fire, he took his shovel and bravely went up to the car, planning to smother any hot spots. He began to pick away at what he hoped was sand, but it turned out to be hard sandstone and he wasn't able to bring up a single grain, not able to help in this way...wanting to be so helpful and looking so helpless.

I remember that for me it turned out to be a "Lucy and Desi" incident indeed, because that night you could have seen me running like a gazelle down the alley. And Bill's mother, Grandma (Mildred) Abbott, who lived in a little studio nextdoor to our house, was also in attendance, behind me, running as fast as she could. We had been having dinner before the accident and had left the house in a big hurry. Later,

13

after the activity had ceased, we looked down and saw that her shoes were on the wrong feet! Of course, after all the urgency and tension we broke up with laughter.

Larry Good, who lived with his family on the beach at about 20th Street, was usually awakened by the same crash noises as we were, and he would arrive from around the corner — also to help. One of Larry's houses on the beach was the one Jimmy Durante leased each year. Later Larry's daughter Susie Stevenson and her family lived in that house until it was sold through my firm (how exciting for me!) and replaced with a splendid contemporary architect-designed residence with a value of somewhat over 20 million dollars!

A practical solution for coastal living

Over the same years we lived on Coast Boulevard, the two Mannen brothers and their families also lived there. Paul Mannen served on the 22nd Agricultural District Board of Directors at that time. His brother Fred was a Deputy Sheriff. Later Fred's son Frank told me their house had originally been moved from elsewhere onto its Coast Boulevard site. It is my understanding after my conversations with some of the old-timers, that a couple of other houses had been moved to sites in the Beach Colony as well (Larry Good's house and Stuart Shore's). How convenient and practical it was!

A personal lesson in Del Mar real estate

I remember when, after a few years in Del Mar, we wanted to buy the house we were renting from the old timer who owned it, and another one of the local people said to me, "You poor dumb girl. You're not going to pay $22,000 for that?!"

We didn't really have that much money, and being so naive and insecure, as many were, we had no concept of trying to get the house for less. We did raise enough to put $19,000 into a house, but we had to go north to Cardiff to find one for that price. Oh my, how sad for us.

And this experience led me to the quiet philosophy I developed later, which I still adhere to, about what an important role a real estate professional can, and should, play in the lives of people and their investment in their purchases, to be sure they feel competent and are well informed!

Chapter 3

A Del Mar education

Our two sons, Mark and Nick, attended Del Mar Elementary School during the last year of the "Niemann dynasty," Principal Ruth Niemann's last year before retirement. She was followed by Clark Howard, the new principal and also Del Mar Union School District superintendent. Well, he became as popular and respected as Ruth, maybe even more so, as she had never been seen driving the school bus, as Clark did from time to time!

In the 1950s Del Mar Elementary School was located on the school site at 9th Street. It was not too many blocks away for our boys to walk

Nick (left) and Mark Abbott in their elementary school days, wearing shirts sewn by their mother, Chiquita

15

or ride their bikes to it. I also recall the site where the kids played — the Shores property right near the school. It was just naturally there for the children to use and play on.

Learning to save

School lunches were 25 cents; we could not afford them every day, so we sent the boys with their lunch money once or twice a week. One week I received a call: "Chiquita, doesn't Nick have any money for lunch?"

"Yes."

"Well, he's not eating lunch, and I discovered that he's been putting the money in his school bank account." Bank of America had a program through the schools that helped kids learn the value of saving money. And, no kidding, Nick really was banking his lunch money.

Anticipating the future

I remember once while our boys were attending Del Mar Elementary, Clark told me the following story while we were standing outside a classroom. It seemed unbelievable. He pretended to pull something from his shirt pocket as he said, "Chiquita, one of these days the boys will not have to use a pencil and paper to add and subtract. They will have this little device — yep, here it is: an electronic gadget with others to come." He referenced a calculator, and that was in 1956.

A partnership of trust

Clark Howard was also a very logical businessman who was investing in real estate, which could be a very practical practice. Well, later, when I worked as a realtor, he bought, through me, a small duplex on Coast Boulevard to live in during the school year. Clark Howard was my first and loyal client.

Thereafter, when the University of California, San Diego (UCSD) came into being, he and I gave student renters the benefit of the doubt; he trusted the first ones, believing they would take good care of his property. How thrilling for me! Would this be the start of student winter rentals? Maybe UCSD students were special. We called it a partnership of trust, and it worked well for years. This was my way — to trust all parties, and I have been lucky to be able to continue to work in this fashion. To this day an occasional former student will call or drop by just to say hello. I collect photos of their families.

That trusting part of Clark as well as the caliber of education he fostered really led to my success in the local real estate business for years and years. I was able to sell houses to parents because of the superior education their children would receive through the Del Mar schools. I did keep telling Clark this for many years afterwards while we both simply kept on doing the same thing. To this day Del Mar's popularity results partly from superior schools.

Beyond Del Mar Elementary

Del Mar Elementary provided great preparation for the years to come in the schools of the San Dieguito Union High School District. We were living in Cardiff during those years, and both Mark and Nick graduated from San Dieguito High School (now San Dieguito Academy).

A snapshot taken on Mark's high-school graduation day, outside our home in Cardiff (left to right, Nick, Chiquita, grandmother Mildred Abbott, and Mark)

Chapter 4
Life in the village

Our Beach Colony neighborhood was almost devoid of activity for most of the year. I recall that days after our arrival there, some creative person in town thought it would be fun to close Coast Boulevard and put on a big party with food — a street dance, or fiesta, while the summer people were still around to enjoy it. A few of the neighbors were members of the Del Mar Civic Association (it was founded by property owners in the beach area — I think I still have a copy of their charter). And it was undoubtedly some of these folks who came up with the idea.

Well, Fiesta Del Mar took place. "We" closed the road. Was a permit required? I seriously doubt any of us even thought of it. We were not a city yet — who ever asked for permission in those days? Large Mexican hats and festive colorful garb were the costume for the event. With lots of food and dancing, and loud music filling the air, a really good time was the result! Over the years, when some of us have yearned for a repeat performance, somehow the word "permit" to close the street was always heard, often along with "Del Mar, an incorporated city" and so on.

A developing center of commercial activity

The fiesta was held during the period when Nick Giordano had his drugstore. Please picture yourself driving south on Highway 101 coming out of the Beach Colony area where we lived. You start up the hill, with Coast Boulevard lying 40 to 50 feet lower than that section of 101, which would later be called Camino Del Mar, though in 1956 it was still just "the highway" to us. As the road flattened out, you entered the "town," which boasted the old Hotel Del Mar and a small coffee shop or two, with Nick Giordano's Del Mar Drugs and Gleason's Dry Goods on the corner of 15th Street.

Later the town would be home to Carlos & Annie's (and still later Randy Gruber's Americana Restaurant); Bill Owen's Del Mar Market in that Tudor building on the corner; a liquor store (Zel's Liquor was 10 or more years later); and a restaurant known as Victor's Prime Rib (and after that, Bully's).

A painting of the building at the north end of the town, on the southwest corner of 15th Street and Highway 101 (now Camino Del Mar), by Del Mar artist Vilma Malmberg

Working at Nick Giordano's drugstore in the early days of our lives in Del Mar was a wonderful pharmacist, George Kendall. George's wife, Eleanor, was an educator and outgoing, but George was exceptionally quiet. A tall, thin man, he walked very slowly down Coast Boulevard from 22nd Street, where they lived, to 15th Street, where the drugstore was and where he dispensed drugs in the same easy fashion ... and maybe a candy bar or two. Everyone loved him.

I remember the market. Bill Owen of the Del Mar Market kept our kids honest — no stolen candy bars or your mother gets a call! That's the kind of thing that made it a village, and Bill Owen did that for us.

The Tudor building on the corner of 15th Street changed hands several times. Before Jim Watkins bought it, there was a restaurant and bar on the first floor and living apartments upstairs. Not a great mix. Fortunately, when Jim bought the building its use was changed (it was not easy) into what we have today — mini office suites, not living apartments, on the second floor, and little shops, the source of memories of pleasant hours, on the first floor. Jim Watkins, and then Anne Mery, operated Earth Song Books, and Virginia Igonda had the Ocean Song Gallery. Colorful window displays, music and two lovely ladies, colorful in their own right, bringing us entertaining and thoughtful experiences, and books we not only enjoyed but may even return to. Today Anne Mery's eCeltic Books & Treasures exists inside Julie's Beach Life, at the same address where Earth Song used to be.

Also in one of those first-floor spaces, Carol Watkins opened her ice cream shop. She had always wanted one there, and she got it when Jim Watkins bought the building. Later Carol sold the operation to Chuck Benson for Annie, his wife, who also had always wanted an ice cream store. At the time, Chuck worked as a real estate agent for my firm, Chiquita Abbott Real Estate, and was known for his dapper way of dressing. How were we to know that one day — rather soon, in fact — he would trade in that white shirt and tie for a cowboy hat and rename himself "Carlos" (of Carlos & Annie's restaurant of Del Mar fame), a name he carried with him to Santa Fe, New Mexico, where they relocated.

The "good ol' days" in Del Mar

We should return to Mr. Gleason, the variety store owner, at the time we met him in the late 1950s. When he discovered the Abbotts were to be permanent residents — not summer people — he greeted me more warmly. In those days we were too young to understand and appreciate the fact that some of the residents had owned property in Del Mar much, much longer, and they, not we, were really the natives!

Back then Del Mar still had a pier, and my boys bicycled down there and were able to spend time with the neighborhood fishermen; they even got to enjoy a hamburger served from the "pergola" sandwich shack, which was very close by. I remember that so many young people used to go often to the pergola, and now even though they're pretty senior, it's still remembered with fondness.

No longer do we have a pergola. It was "traded in" for Jake's Del Mar and the Poseidon — with many more restaurants located up and down Camino Del Mar today. What a mecca we've become for restaurant goers!

Looking north through the structure that housed "the pergola" snack shop when we first came to Del Mar. This photo was taken after the pergola had been vacated but before the powerhouse was renovated.

Chapter 5
Getting to know Del Mar

It seems to me that Del Mar in the 1950s was like Monrovia in the 1930s, when I was growing up. I guess I never thought about the name of "Grand Avenue," the street in Monrovia where we played kick the can, until I entered the real estate field years later in Del Mar and learned that streets are often named after a famous or well-known person (perhaps the one who developed the area) or after some local feature. The street named Grand led up the hillside toward a then very well known tuberculosis treatment center called Pottenger Sanatorium. (The mind is incredible in calling up otherwise long forgotten things!) The street must have been given the name "Grand" because it was main or wide or long or important.

When my family, luckily, landed on Coast Boulevard in Del Mar, the street was pretty empty of traffic, as Monrovia's Grand Avenue had been in the '30s. Down the street there was the old powerhouse — abandoned at that point, and not yet restored. Years later I was attending a meeting of the Board of Directors of Friends of the Powerhouse when I looked up and there was Frank Mannen, whom I had met years before. Both of us had been involved for months helping Barbara Harper and our other volunteers ask for and collect funds for the renovation of the powerhouse. How sweet it was when Barbara felt we had collected enough to start the work. No way that building will require any more maintenance in our lifetimes!

The music of Del Mar
Before the powerhouse was restored, it was pretty dismal, but someone had arranged for some Dixieland guys to meet down there and play some gigs. There was one trombonist who played barefoot using his feet. What was his name? Sonny!

Today, because of the efforts of Friends of the Powerhouse, Del Mar residents and visitors can enjoy the Powerhouse Park and Beach and the restored Del Mar Powerhouse Community Center (upper right), a venue for special events.

We had friends around here who played with some of the popular bands of the time and later with little groups in La Jolla, through the '80s. Our area is loaded with professional talent. Think of the people I got to meet. It's so exciting.

You know, since our arrival, Del Mar has brought forth some fine professional musicians — local kids all grown up. Peter Sprague and his brother Tripp, Rob Schneiderman, Steve Feierabend, Mark Lessman, Bryant Allard, and of course Bim Strasberg, who later played in New York clubs. Would they have done so well had they not had the tutelage of UCSD Professor Bert Turetzky, a Del Mar resident for many years?

What is a kid without a mom with patience and time like June Strasberg, Carol Harrington, Barbara Schneiderman, Rosalind Lorwin Feierabend, Pauline Lessman and Irmgard Allard, along with other parents who must have lived through those periods of "ooh! ooh!" until the sounds turned to be "ahh...ahh..."

After these musicians and their patient parents came others — Paul and Eric Keeling, and still later, Steve Denyes and Brendan Kremer. Pals from kindergarten onward, Steve and Brendan grew up to become Hullabaloo, a band nationally recognized for its "free-range, organic, kid folk music," bringing joy to children and parents alike.

You must know I love just being here.

The start of a career

Living in paradise is wonderful, but after a bit I needed to become more a part of the Del Mar community. I always listened to the advice of my mother-in-law, Mildred Abbott, to whom I could relate. Together we decided we would seek real estate licenses and really learn about the area. So that's what we did.

My only previous experience in the real estate business had been a job on Balboa Island, where my boss owned a beachfront house. I rather looked after it from time to time, so I could stretch that experience and say I had managed it, though in truth it was never rented. I then became more involved in his purchase of a Valley Center ranch that had belonged to Fred Astaire, and this helped round out my real estate experience. Much career development really did take place on this one.

At the time we decided to get into real estate, an agent (licensed to help people buy, sell or rent real estate) had to work two years as a licensee before being eligible to become a broker (licensed to own a real estate firm and hire agents); there were no shortcuts. I got my first license in 1958, and I was on my way.

The BB gun, Marcella Rabwin and Desi Arnaz's house

In the 1960s I learned that Del Mar Race Track was home not only to thoroughbred horses but also to a group of trotter horses that were here for their winter season. While their parents were here with the horses, some of their youngsters came along, and so a new playmate for our young son Nick appeared on the scene. Since very few children lived in the Beach Colony during the winter, we were pleased — although the friend brought with him a BB gun, which was on the forbidden list in our home. Nevertheless, Nick did use his friend's gun one day while they were playing on the beach. When the two boys lay on the wide stretch of sand in between 19th and 21st Streets, Nick shot toward the few homes way back from where they were lying, and he hit the big plate-glass window of an older gentleman named Sanderson.

Well, I was notified, and we seemed to be the only parents responding to the complaint. The cost to replace the glass was a whopping $40. Horrors! (My mind says maybe it was $400; after all, this home was a beach mansion.) And Bill Abbott was an educator and still taking graduate classes; he and a colleague drove back and forth twice a week to

University of Southern California (USC) using that horrible road. We did not have a spare $400 (or even a spare $40), so we made arrangements to pay over several months.

Okay, the incredible finish to this story of the house with the shot-out window is that years later, as my career in real estate was under way, I was approached by Desi Arnaz through the personal referral of Marcella Rabwin. (What a fascinating lady she was. Her history included working directly for Cecil B. DeMille as a child.) She was married to a very popular and successful M.D. to the stars, Dr. Marcus Rabwin. They made their summer (go-to-the-races) home on Ocean Front. It was a fabulous place to entertain the stars, of course. That very property continues today to attract a special ownership.

Anyway, after Marcella Rabwin had introduced us, Desi and I could be found peeking into the windows of the locked-up old houses in the Beach Colony. "Let's walk down the beach and look," he said. So off we went, and we were at the water's edge when he stopped in front of a very large home in the distance (imagine all that sand and very few houses). He pointed at this big house close to the Rabwin house. It was the very house that Nick had shot the window out of.

Oh, my, another wave of horror went through me as I learned that my charge was to walk up to the front door and tell the owner that the man standing on the beach in front of his home wanted to buy it. As luck would have it, someone was in the house. And much to my surprise, this gentleman said, "OK, if he wants to pay twice what it's worth." I was so inexperienced; I turned around and fought my way back through the deep sand to Desi and repeated the man's reply verbatim. Desi said "OK." What to do now?

We slowly made our way back to my little convertible and drove to town to my office, where his driver and limousine were waiting to take him back to his office. We agreed to talk later. Meanwhile I would prepare his papers. I did have the presence of mind to remember the name of the title company (there were but two in San Diego at the time). Can you imagine? And Desi was so polite but still didn't pronounce my name correctly — never did. Did I care — of course not! Anyway, the price turned out to be $150,000 cash.

Another incredible thing about this deal was that Desi later asked the seller, Mr. Sanderson, to carry the note for a short while — can you imagine? — and he did! And even more incredible is that the seller and I went to the title company in person (with his driver), and escrow was completed within 24 hours. Perhaps that had something to do with Mr. Sanderson reminding the title officer that they were always so slow getting escrows closed, so they were on alert. Still another surprise was to learn that this man, Mr. Sanderson, had built early residential developments in Kearny Mesa in San Diego and in Borrego Springs as well … so new to me.

Chapter 6

Becoming a part of the community

Being the mother of my two wonderful boys, I was able to be a part of their childhood in Del Mar, from squeezing lemons for that weekly ballgame to driving them to cotillion, with much in between. The name Don Benjamin soon became a household word, for his dance lessons included instruction not only for the children but for the parents as well. Before long the entire family was on the dance floor. A whole company of dancers was created in our sleepy little community during those years!

Sponsors and volunteers

You must know that Del Mar parents can do anything — maybe not all smoothly all the time, but they are all willing to try. An amazing village. Many of the local business people sponsored kids' organizations: scouts, baseball, cotillion and others. In Del Mar I was able to grow professionally. My husband spent almost all his waking moments between greater Los Angeles "picking up a few more units" toward his PhD, and "selling guidance" in San Diego County.

My boys really loved living here. There was Little League baseball (Pony League was just being introduced). They became involved with Boy Scouts as well. And it was through their activities that I became involved in the community. You know, PTA and school sports are instrumental in keeping parents involved. And then you do the hot dog bit, right? (Then, not now. Fast-food spots were later prohibited by ordinance in "our village"!)

I personally squeezed lemons brought by a wonderful person from Rancho Santa Fe who gave all of us lemons from his grove. We had a big freezer, where we would store some juice, and just before each game, we would pack up large quantities of juice, sugar and water — and hope there would be someone who could help carry it all from the

27

car to the field, and stay long enough to help serve the lemonade and barbecue the hot dogs. Our friend and dance and etiquette teacher, Don Benjamin, and I were elected by default. I remember when the actor Victor Mature was to throw out the first ball of the season in a Rancho Santa Fe game, and my kids were so very impressed.

Anyway, to continue, volunteers were desperately needed to help with the serving and cleanup of the equipment to make this vital activity happen. So, I called the mothers of whatever children I had telephone numbers for.

One of my first calls was to the Steve Farrell family, and since it was he who answered, I innocently asked if he could be a volunteer to assist in transporting all the lemonade and equipment to the ball field. How was I to know that it was he — a rare building contractor living in Del Mar — who had been the one man with big equipment that could sweep or clear the weedy fields…and who had been doing so for a number of years. Oops, this telephone call was quite unsuccessful. He was doing a lot for the team already.

Years after I had become a real estate agent, I met Steve Farrell in person, and again I did not handle things well. I had driven the neighborhood and discovered a house being built. I called up to the man standing on the roof to ask him if I could talk to him about a listing contract when the house was completed. I guess

he was reluctant, but he did climb down, handed me a set of plans and proceeded to climb back up. Oops. I was a new licensee whose experience had been as an executive secretary for a big-city industrialist, and I had never read a set of plans.

Life is strange and wonderful, for again, years later, Steve Farrell and I met under different circumstances, and we were married to each other for 47 years. I learned he was not always so disturbed by volunteers who continued to ask him for either money or energy!

Chiquita Abbott Farrell and Steve Farrell many years later

28

Getting the lay of the land

The north part of San Diego County consisted in large part of agriculture or Navy personnel, as they played such large parts here. Most of the hillsides were covered with strawberries grown by local farmers. The fields were gradually replaced by houses.

Solana Beach, just north of Del Mar, was the lucky home of a firm from Ohio called Bill Jack Scientific Instruments, named after founder Bill Jack, who settled in Solana Beach with his family. I believe the company was the largest employer in the area at the time. Their plant was housed in the quonset huts on South Cedros Avenue, now home to the Belly Up Tavern and so many small businesses in the Cedros Design District. Their presence brought families who intended to stay, and they began to buy or build modest homes on the hill, where views of the sea were the norm. Some of these people and their families are still living in our area as our friends and neighbors.

Andrew Kay, a brilliant engineer, founded Non-Linear Systems (NLS), an electronics manufacturing company, in Solana Beach. The first digital multimeter was manufactured by NLS, and NLS founded Kaypro Corporation, which designed and produced the Kaypro, one of the early desktop computers. Andrew's daughter Janice and her husband, Michael Batter, have designed and built many of Del Mar's contemporary homes through their architectural firm, Batter Kay Associates. (They also restored and remodeled the original cottage on the grounds of the old Hotel Del Mar.)

Chapter 7

Starting out in real estate

Remember that in the 1950s Del Mar basically consisted of small two-bedroom cottages, many of them lived in by Navy people who would come into town during the end of their duty, or ultimately retire here. Most of the larger homes came later, the result of new family needs, with a couple of notable exceptions that anyone with an interest in Del Mar real estate would quickly become aware of.

The Castle

One of the larger homes we learned about was the Castle on Avenida Primavera. It was pretty impressive at the time it was built in 1925 for Ruth and Marston Harding, and it still is today. There are so many fun stories to tell about the Castle and the families who owned and lived in it. The owner in the 1950s, Calvin McGaugh, had a hosiery manufacturing firm and operated it from the site that's now Jake's Del Mar restaurant. I remember that one of his sons was named Prince.

At about 10,000 square feet including a detached guest house, the Castle itself was decorated with traditional regal furnishings as it should be — so fascinating for those of us who were able to visit and climb to the top of the tower. It transferred from the McGaughs to the Kaufmans to Sandy Shapery to Tony Robbins; then it went back into Shapery's ownership. Ralph and Laura DeMarco purchased it and have raised their family there. (Laura became one of the most dedicated and capable historians in our midst.)

It's important to be reminded that there were rough economic years during the above ownerships, and that people's wealth and lifestyle are so dependent on the greater economy. To become an owner of the Castle carried with it the recognition of being a special individual or family with a large discretionary income, because the selling price at each transaction was definitely a lot of money! It has continued to be a totally fascinating property, and it sits on one of Del Mar's highest spots.

The Del Mar Castle as it looked in 1996

The "Snakewall" property

Speaking of Del Mar's large historic homes, along with the Castle there's the "Snakewall" property. The ownership records show approximately 19 acres inside that wall, consisting of 13 legal lots and miscellaneous structures throughout.

Like the Castle, the Snakewall property has many stories to tell. The land was bought by the owner of the Monolith Portland Cement company, Coy Burnett, in the 1920s. The story goes that he built the wall that surrounds the entire property in order to keep out rattlesnakes. But that story has been pretty well debunked by his granddaughter Brier Miller Minor in her memoir and local history, *Walking the Wall: Life Behind Del Mar's "Snakewall."* Larry Brooks, president of the Del Mar Historical Society, was involved in gathering history about the early family and the property as well.

The Burnetts named the estate "La Atalaya," the watchtower. The site included a large home on top of the hill, accessed from the very top

31

of the circle on Serpentine Drive. It included a number of buildings to house the help as well as the farm animals (chickens and horses) down below, and a garden — a veritable self-contained estate. In the early 1940s the home located on top of the hill suffered a fire that destroyed a large part of it, which the Burnett family never rebuilt.

After Mr. Burnett's death in 1971, the family sold the property to James Smith, who spent considerable energy and money on development plans for a large resort hotel. What extravagant plans! But they were never approved by the City of Del Mar.

The present owners, Ron and Lucille Neeley, have maintained the large stand of Torrey pine trees on the property. They cleared the burn site and built a large home there — a masterpiece of design. They made many other improvements to the property, including planting an olive tree grove. Ron Neeley told me that at the time of rebuilding and renovating the estate, the total project was the largest engineering job ever on the books of the City of Del Mar.

PHOTO: BRIER MILLER MINOR / FROM WALKING THE WALL: LIFE BEHIND DEL MAR'S "SNAKEWALL" / USED WITH PERMISSION

The "Snakewall" property today, viewed from the east

The state of real estate at mid-century

Now for another perhaps enlightening review of my real estate education and background. Because there was mostly vacant land in Del Mar in the 1950s, we needed to learn how to read legal descriptions where measurements were broken down by engineering terms of *metes and bounds,* the boundaries of a parcel of real estate as identified by its natural landmarks, a system used all over the world. Real estate agents also had to know how to appraise and how to read plans. I suspect there is little emphasis on that today, since title companies do that job for agents. But we did have to learn those skills at that time, and some of us were seen in high-heeled shoes tramping among the weeds, to locate what we perceived to be block corners in the Del Mar Heights subdivision.

At the time there was no water to the area, no access to gas or electricity. There were those of us agents who worked to gather enough signatures to put together a 1911-Act bond to achieve the development of services to the property, but it was a long time before it was completed.

Also, in those days there was, of course, no computer to use. Copy machines were rare — we had carbon paper for making copies of typed or handwritten documents, and we reproduced maps by taping them onto a glass door in my office and hand-copying them onto tracing paper. We went down to the County offices, where we were allowed to copy from their ownership books, where county deeds were recorded. And that's the way we kept track of every transaction in Del Mar — yes, it is. I could go on and on!

For instance, when I wanted to know the history of some land when Fairbanks Ranch was being developed, and about Douglas Fairbanks himself, I had to go to a basement area beneath one of commercial buildings in the city of San Diego — called "the morgue." There I was given some microfiche to read. That was an adventure! This was the first time I had used microfiche, and it even included some legal court records as I recall.

All right, onward with my real estate education and background. There was just a lot of vacant land, and we were selling lots and some acreage and learning how to read legal descriptions. We needed to know a little about building basics, so we learned that too.

Keep in mind that the property lines of many Del Mar lots are very irregular (following the contours of the hill, for instance), and so we absolutely needed to be able to read those legal descriptions so we could point buyers to their new sites, or at least to the corner pins put there by the civil engineers who did the surveys. The only engineering company in our area that we used was Rancho Santa Fe Engineers.

Chapter 8

The real estate business evolves

I remember when the shopping strip that later was the original Del Mar Plaza so nicely housed the florist shop run by Peg and Lee Cantley (who later owned Lion in the Sun), a small dress shop, a barber shop, Chiquita Abbott Realtors, a stock brokerage firm, Zel's liquor store, Jonathan's Market at one point, California Bank and Trust, and the Del Mar branch of the San Diego County Library. It was always so very busy up there, but with adequate parking space, so parking was never an issue.

Let me relate an incident that happened while our business was located there. My agent Donna Lilly was meeting at our office with a well-known author from La Jolla. Donna was so excited, but had the presence of mind to ask why he had come to us. He said quite simply, "Because there was parking."

Ooh … what heartbreak for me. I was so wanting to hear the words "Because of your brokerage"!

For 20 years Chiquita Abbott Realtors operated out of an office in the Del Mar Plaza, a "shopping strip" at 15th Street and Camino Del Mar (or Highway 101 as it was called in the early days).

Oh, well, this story could have been relayed to the City fathers and mothers of Del Mar years later, with another nudge to get adequate parking on the City's own site! (Whoa — in 2019 they did it!)

It was wonderful being on the hill up there, with beautiful views from all over the Plaza, and our little firm having the use of a great deck with a parklike setting and a view of the trees on the hills of Del Mar. Our space was small, but I was still so apprehensive about the rent being $150 per month. (Would I really make enough sales to warrant that?) We worked hard, but perhaps it was made easier because we knew so many people in the village.

The Plaza was owned by two of the Fletcher family (Steve and Pete) and Terry Lingenfelder, their brother-in-law. They also developed the beach area known as Sandy Lane, as well as Flower Hill Shopping Center. I remember Steve personally bringing us a big box of grapefruit from his ranch in Borrego each holiday season. This is a small town, and personal relationships continue for many of us in Del Mar.

Chiquita Abbott Realtors enjoying the patio behind their Del Mar Plaza office (left to right, Margaret McIntosh, Julie Pinney, June Mauer, Chiquita Abbott, Nancy Rinehart, Harry Stebner, Phyllis Healy, Jean Buckley, Jane Anderson)

A big investment in the latest technology

After about 20 years in Del Mar Plaza, I moved my office to 1234 Camino Del Mar, sharing the building with Phil Jefferson and his insurance business. When I made the move, I felt I was very much on the leading edge as a "boutique" agency, with our own identity and more prestige.

And so I went to the big City of San Diego, sought out the big firm of IBM, and bought a computer. I even paid $15,000 for it! Could I say I "chose" it? No way. Keep in mind I knew nothing about computers, just what I had read in the ads, but I knew they were designed to help with organizing.

It was $4.00 per hour for my secretary to learn how to use it. So we did only that one initial hour, no more.

Another lesson learned: The young salesman said to me "What do you want it to do for you?" How would *I* know?! Why did he not sit down and tell me what his great machines could really do? And what to expect if we needed help? As it turned out, we had to learn about it ourselves.

Continuing with my goal of being "first," we invested in pagers. I was only somewhat familiar with what pagers could do for us. Jim Healy, husband of my agent Phyllis Healy, was selling the Executone System. I had confidence in him, and so I simply bit the bullet and did it.

"Whoa ..." my agents told me afterwards, "I'm not going to be tied down to this."

But we gradually learned that the paging system gave us *more* freedom, not less. Because we could always be reached, we could be in other places doing other things. No longer did we have to sit in the office, wait, and when the phone rang, put up our hands and say, "I'll get it!" I won the pager round — whew!

Reflect with me for a moment. I had been on the hill in the Del Mar Plaza 20 years, and it took that long for this new equipment to find its way to us. And I am still a traditionalist. Along with computers, scanners, printers and even iPhones, to this day I also have an original IBM Selectric typewriter for those special needs — completely renovated by a very mature, experienced mechanic.

Growing

As our intrepid band of talented agents grew, I recruited my elder son Mark to be part of the organization. He let me know that he had no enthusiasm for selling *per se*, but he brought managerial skills and a wonderful sense of organization to the company.

Chiquita Abbott Real Estate, Inc. at 1234 Camino Del Mar. The "boutique" agency shared the site with the Philip B. Jefferson Insurance Agency until Phil retired. Standing at far left is Mark Abbott, Vice President of the corporation. Among others in this photo are Julie Pinney, Alyson Goudy, Chiquita Abbott, Joe Gallo, Donna Lilly and Sherry Shriver.

We were learning and we worked hard. Much later, as a perk, only one or two agents in my firm (Julie Pinney and Phyllis Healy) received a cell phone from me because of their outstanding record of successful transactions. At the time that was a big deal!

Right here in Del Mar

Thinking about cell phones, one of our local residents and a personal friend, Martin Cooper, is known all over the world as the "father of the cell phone," invented during his tenure at Motorola. He was awarded the highest honor in communications technology, the Marconi Prize, in 2013.

His wife's dad really started the paging industry, I believe, and she, Arlene Harris, is also an expert in the field of communication. Theirs is a continuing story of worldwide acclaim. Recognizing the incredible growth of our senior population with an ever increasing need for good telephone service, Arlene Harris originated the GreatCall telephone system (now Lively) with an inexpensive, easy-to-use cell phone called the Jitterbug.

I'm reminded that back in the late 1920s, my own dad wired the first intercity telephone board for the small Southern California cities of Monrovia, Arcadia and Duarte for California Water & Telephone. And now almost 100 years later, we have smartphones — Android, iPhone — and an abundance of other electronic devices.

What's next? Marty Cooper once told me he could envision a day when all of us would have personal chips inserted under our skin that would serve as access to perhaps a large database of all types of information. I have to think of it this way: Look at all that's happened during my lifetime — what a period I've lived in. And it looks like communication and access to information may be about to break loose again.

Chapter 9
The growth of Del Mar

From the time I was first introduced to Del Mar in the 1950s, back when most of the area contained just small two-bedroom cottages lived in by retired Navy personnel, I was aware of the intrigue created by the area's unique geography. Rising almost like a volcano, the land runs from sea level to some 350 feet of elevation, all within a couple of miles. Of course, combined with its sandy beaches, its views of the sea and the mild weather, this geography creates an air of privacy that makes the place nearly perfect.

Because of this God-given gift, Del Mar has always had great international appeal, and therefore it enjoyed outside influences from people who had seen much of the world and could really appreciate Del Mar's geography when they encountered it.

New residents
By 1959, Del Mar had decided to incorporate as a city. The new City of Del Mar soon gained new residents. The General Atomic division of General Dynamics, for instance, was built by recruiting very bright scientists from other areas. And likewise, just south of Del Mar the University of California, San Diego (UCSD) was established in 1960, absorbing the Scripps Institution of Oceanography down below it at the beach, and bringing with it a nucleus of new people who established homes in Del Mar. This influx of people was important in the growth of our wonderful army of volunteers, whose interests run the gamut from the environment to social services and cultural programs.

Let us not forget what the behavioral sciences brought to our community. Western Behavioral Sciences Institute of La Jolla, for instance, provided Del Mar with our own Garry Shirts, a continuous resource and vital part of human development analysis, and founder of Simulation Training Systems. We were also to see the development and publication of the magazine *Psychology Today,* started in 1967. The people who made it happen — a new breed with diverse attitudes — became a part of our city. *Psychology Today* founder Nick Charney is an example. By 1981 the magazine had a circulation of over a million. When the successful publication moved its operations to New York City, several of the editorial and design staff opted to remain in Del Mar and surrounding communities, forming the nucleus of a vibrant publishing services industry.

Medical advances and the growing population cried out for the finest of hospital care, schools for the children of these newcomers, and of course, art and music organizations. And so we have it all!

But as these institutions were being built in the 1960s, '70s and '80s, the new families required larger homes. My, what an opportunity for all of our local architects!

Don Schoell, a young architect, came to me looking for a site where he could create a "design" he could showcase. It had to be "the most difficult lot to design and build on." Yep, we finally found it and, as he told me and others, the house had to be redesigned twice before it could be built, because the houses to the east of him had been sold a couple of times and he had to be concerned about not infringing upon their owners' views. Today we realize that he was correct in his approach, for upon completion of this project, he was definitely on his way.

Before this new approach to building took hold in Del Mar, there was a need for enlarging some of our small bungalows from two bedrooms to four or more. But there were problems.

The first problem was that although using architects to design additions was the approach many young homeowners were taking, there were only so many houses in Del Mar that could be remodeled by adding space.

The second problem was that Del Mar had stiff ordinances about land use, which had to be adhered to. A major constraint was complying with "FAR" — that is, Floor Area Ratio, which is the ratio between the square footage of the building and the size of the lot it's being built on. So many lots in Del Mar are of varying shapes, sizes and topography, and meeting the challenges of both the ordinances and the lot configurations was quite an undertaking — thus the huge need for trained architects. In many cases the irregularly shaped lots created hardships, and larger houses were impossible.

The legacy of Herb Turner

Herbert B. Turner always had a way of making things seem easy — or at least making them happen without fanfare. Oh, what fond memories that brings to mind. In those times of changes in Del Mar, there were not too many active professional relationships that survived the years. But I like to feel that my relationship with Herb was one that did.

Herb was a great designer, one with a philosophy that preached "simple, straightforward, but mostly of nature." He was able to incorporate the great outdoors in the residences he designed, often using materials or building approaches pretty much untried before. He found ways of providing privacy within natural environments. His forte was to find a piece of land, then design something that would fit perfectly. He did this, for instance, with the homes he designed between 7th and 8th Streets on the hill. He was so fanatical about natural, meaning un-landscaped, that he was known to forbid his subcontractors to walk on any of the wild weeds or to bring in equipment that caused disturbance.

My agents were to locate a buyer for each home (but not too fast), and the buyer simply had to be willing to live without green grass! There was a time when Herb was critical of us because we had located a family too soon, and he would not be hurried!

Then there was the 10-unit Playa Del Mar gated condominium community in the Beach Colony. Once again, Herb would not be rushed;

The condominiums in Herb Turner's Playa Del Mar gated community on the east side of Highway 101 were designed with built-in vacuums and two fireplaces.

41

not even his backer/partner Will Hopper was allowed to hurry him. I am still so thrilled about being able to choose the wooden sign for Playa Del Mar, perhaps because I paid for it.

To add a bit of humor to these memories of Herb, I tell the story of those times and how scarce money was. Herb was always so loyal, using my firm as his realtor for all his business, that a couple of times, when cash was short, I did without my fee, and from time to time I even advanced a bit to Herb. Well, this one time we agreed that he would pay me a little each month — no interest — simply pay me back over time. The payments went on for a couple of years, and then one day I referred to my books and *whoa!* — I now owed Herb some money. He had overpaid and neither of us had noticed! That gave each of us a warm and fuzzy, though foolish, feeling! Of course we laughed, and I paid him back!

Del Mar spreading east

Down the street — just beyond the eastern border of our incorporated city of Del Mar, and still within the same elementary and secondary school districts — lay the old subdivision called Del Mar Heights, which is now within the boundaries of the city of San Diego. Most of the lots were designed to have regular rectangular borders, to be 50 feet by 140 feet, with alleys, and with building guidelines far less restrictive than within the city of Del Mar. By building outside the Del Mar city limits, new residents would be able to enjoy the same Del Mar lifestyle at a lower cost and with fewer building constraints. For all these reasons, the south developed in a way that tended to be more child-oriented.

When the Del Mar Heights land was first subdivided, there had been no utilities to the lots. But a petition based on the Improvement Act of 1911 had caused the lots to be assessed for such improvements as utility services, and the property owners at that time agreed to such long-term assessments.

I began to sell these lots, which became increasingly easier, because by the 1960s and '70s the utilities were in place. I sold some with western ocean views for $3000, and even $4000. Those on top of the hill and farther east were available for far less. I sold some of those for $2,000.

Even before that time, some daring individuals had bought lots as investments. I was so excited, because I had become aware of the *installment-sale-purchase* vehicle. I began to sell lots for a 29% down payment with monthly payments for the balance, making sure the buyer held the property for at least three years to comply with the rules. Most sellers did demand payoff by the end of three years, but at that point the buyer could acquire a mortgage. Figure: $3,000 minus 29% (or $870) down, leaving a balance of $2130; with a mortgage, payments could be amortized over 30 years, which resulted in monthly payments like $12.71 (including interest and taxes).

The name I gave the area was "New Del Mar," as differentiated from the incorporated area, which I then referred to as Old Del Mar (but not *Olde* Del Mar). Why New Del Mar, you ask? People moving to the area always felt they really did live in Del Mar. Who cared whether it was within the boundaries of the incorporated city? The subdivision that became New Del Mar had been created in 1887 (about the same time that Old Del Mar was also planned and subdivided), and as one looked to the east, there were acres and acres of vacant land.

The real estate business, Del Mar–style

Before I started selling property in Del Mar Heights, I had not been exposed to this type of real estate environment. Let me take you back to the time when, as real estate agents, we were taught how to read plans and figure values, how to appraise by comparison, and how to figure building costs. I suspect there's little emphasis on that today in the brokerage field, since all that work is done by engineers or other specialists. But we did have to learn it at that time.

There were basically no computers, but we had plenty of IBM Selectric typewriters, carbon paper and tracing paper, and as agents we were welcome to use the County Recorder's ownership books, and to copy (by hand) directly from their pages. And that was the way of every transaction in Del Mar. We stood at the counter. Everything was written in long hand — the Palmer method!

The Design Review Board

As a real estate agent, I realized the City of Del Mar was becoming more restless about how things looked. With the changes in the city's cultural climate and demographics, there was an increased concern about the design and esthetics of both commercial buildings and housing. As an agent, I often found myself involved with zoning regulations. And I realized the City was becoming more proactive about zoning, about preventing unexpected changes.

Tom Pearson had a unique way with ideas and people. In the 1960s when he was mayor of Del Mar, he and Jim Watkins came up with the idea of establishing a volunteer Design Review Board on behalf of the City, with a focus on future development. One thing that needed to be addressed, they thought, was the way the little houses being built in the beach neighborhoods resembled cracker boxes; some builders had been putting things up as inexpensively as they could. But attitudes were changing.

There was an eclectic array of houses fronting the ocean in the Beach Colony when the Design Review Board was established.

I was honored when I was invited to be a founding member of the Design Review Board, and I accepted the invitation. Led by Jim Watkins, the members of that first Board came up with a statement of the goals we were trying to achieve. I think people today need to understand that the idea behind the Design Review Board was simply to encourage builders and developers to "take a new look" at the designs and materials they were using in their building projects.

The beach area on the north end was the entrance to our town, so the design review process as applied to residential buildings started with the Beach Colony. But it seemed to me that each succeeding Board became more demanding and their decisions more onerous, pushing owners' time and dollar limits, perhaps not recognizing what was quietly happening.

With the Design Review Board keeping a fairly heavy hand on building activity, learning how to weave one's way through the necessary processes has always been a feat. It's my understanding that architect Herb Turner, with his quiet way of making things go smoothly, developed the first plan (for a couple's new home in the Beach Colony) that was approved on its initial application and presentation.

The review process grew and grew, and more people became more involved. Soon, if the neighbors no longer liked the color brown, then residents who were building or remodeling were willing to use whatever color was necessary to ensure they got their permit. It was not good that they were put in the position of being so anxious to please that they would go with someone else's preferences.

People used to come to my office and say, "Okay, do I have to do it brown?" Or, "Should I choose black?" Eventually I was so disturbed by this that I wrote a letter to the City Council tendering my resignation from the Board. Frankly, I'm not sure whether my reason for resigning was even noticed. But it was most important to me that applicants still have choices and not be presented with absolutes.

Getting it right

There have been years when applicants needed to apply for design review again and again in order to satisfy all the demands of the Board. Perhaps being in a position where using a talented architect or designer paid off with a happy, win-win situation is what left Del Mar with a village filled with smashing properties! It must be noted that as the years have passed, so many volunteers have worked diligently to close each permit application with a very happy homeowner when the job was completed.

As I've mentioned, it's difficult, always, to accomplish unusual things alone. It always takes special people creating special circumstances! Through the years our mayors and city council members, the policy-making segment of the City, have continued to work hard to provide us with the best of their combined judgment in making policies. True, different people are either pleased or displeased by their actions from time to time.

But because it is City staff, not the policy makers, who are charged with implementing the policies and procedures, and because the people of Del Mar are so vocal, we have heard praise for a certain staff member in some situations, but real displeasure over the way information has come over the counter in other instances. Of course, if a resident never wanted to change anything, there was almost never a disagreement with the City. But if a resident did want to change something, you might begin to see evidence of dissatisfaction.

This type of situation creates the need for real estate agents to become involved. We can't just show property and expect our clients to come away happy. Fortunately, it seems that in time we finally got the design review process right.

Chapter 10
Commercial real estate

So many of our residents have had not only their homes but also their professional offices or other businesses in town for many years. This is special, for on leaving their front doorstep, they have been able to choose between walking on down to the sand or water, or unlocking the door to their very own office. What great choices!

My interests, and my clients' needs, moved me to expand from only residential sales to also include the commercial segment from time to time, and I have concentrated mostly on those commercial properties belonging to my Del Mar residential clients. I was able to broker several of the stand-alone buildings in our small downtown district. If you'll "take a walk" with me, I'll introduce you to just a few of Del Mar's great and interesting commercial buildings. Some of these constructions went practically unnoticed for years. But I think it's important to know about them. Their history should be noted and shared with people, just like the history of residences like the Snakewall property and the Castle.

Camino Del Mar as a commercial district

The commercial buildings we see along Camino Del Mar today reflect the completion of our "face lift" of the downtown commercial district. A City-led project of approximately 20 years in discussion and planning, its goal was to make Camino Del Mar a hub for conviviality, business and commerce — a true pedestrian-oriented commercial spot, where stopping for a cup of coffee or a delicious and beautifully presented meal is a pleasant option. Need a bathing suit to use on your surfboard? You can find it here. Or pick up some school pants, tennis shoes, a pair of shorts or slacks. The aim of the project was to put more businesspeople on the street to help make it happen!

A concept ahead of its time

How thrilled I was when Roger DeWeese called me to represent him in the sale of the old garage building on the northwest corner of 13th Street and Camino Del Mar. Oh my, what a rich history it has. Of course, it housed a gasoline station that served the locals for years before it was converted for other uses. Then during Roger's ownership the situation changed, and tenants were acquired. To rent out spaces within that one immense structure turned out to be quite a challenge.

At one time Roger had partners David Winkler, Jim Watkins and Herb Turner, all of whom added their professional input. Keep in mind that the business climate in downtown Del Mar over the years has sometimes been less than vibrant. Anyway, it became necessary to be creative. The partners demonstrated how local artisans could display and sell their art and other offerings in individual spaces, but without dividing walls — a "mart" structure that people would stroll through. They named it the Village Store. The mart was a good idea — a bit early, but it was to come. Witness the Leaping Lotus, Solo and Antiques Warehouse to the north in the Cedros Design District of Solana Beach some years later.

Skipping to the fall of 2019, important shops such as Country Downs had become ensconced in the old garage building. Oh, how we loved that

The gas station that later became a "mart" and then an office building

presence — such luxury. When Sandy Gordon owned Country Downs, we learned that not only did she have marvelous taste in luxury merchandise, but also the way she decorated the interior of the large space made it such an appealing place to shop. Sandy, it turned out, was really a designer who moved temporarily into the role of merchant. Her space included a grand piano and a small kitchen area where she displayed her china, as well as gorgeous linens and housewares. Each Christmas she arranged for me to host my wonderful agents there. I made it a party and arranged for a gift of choice to each attendee. Our offices were just a few feet away, so at dusk we leisurely walked over, strolled around listening to piano music while enjoying scrumptious munchies, and basked in the knowledge that we would each take home a gift.

How sad when we learned that Sandy was giving up half of her space. But who was to replace her? None other than Bill Davidson and his successful firm Davidson Communities. Yes, Del Mar Village was beginning to house other types of industries and tenants. How wonderful it turned out to be to have this equally fine builder sharing the space with Country Downs. We learned that Sandy's other talent was creating interior spaces for custom homes, and she did just that in a home owned by the Davidson family locally.

The purpose of my contract with Roger DeWeese was to negotiate a sale between him and Bill. What a fortuitous match! Roger and his wife could take off on their sailboat and forget his landscape practice, and Bill could house his main office in the renovated old garage building and continue with his most successful enterprises: Davidson Communities, one large residential development after another all over the county.

More from Herb Turner

Driving south into Del Mar on Jimmy Durante Boulevard as you approach the center of town, you will see on your right the space where Herb Turner built a group of wonderful wood and glass buildings called South Fair. This small commercial development, designed and built between 1972 and 1981, offered impressive opportunities for businesses of all types — a true shot in the arm for Del Mar. South Fair included offices, of course, and a restaurant site, but most specially a gallery space and open courtyard where Herb planned for shows of his own art and the work of other artists. Herb's daughter Rachel and son Brent became the keepers

One view of Herb Turner's unique South Fair commercial development

of Herb's marvelous collection of his own formal art — his paintings and the sculptures he did later in his life.

An outstanding office building

There is a smashing all-brick building on the corner of 9th Street and Camino Del Mar, built as office space, and still one of the most luxurious buildings around devoted to office use. Business partners from San Diego gathered up the site and were able to enjoy their own personal suites for several years, and to provide suites for others as well. Such a fine structure.

The Lancor buildings on Camino Del Mar

Architect Joe Lancor designed the contemporary building at 1401 Camino Del Mar for Santa Fe Federal Savings and Loan, where Bob Gavuzzi was brought down to Del Mar as Vice President and Manager. (One day down the road I was able to steal Bob away by encouraging him to join my firm as a real estate licensee.)

Another of Lancor's contemporary buildings, on the corner of 9th Street and Camino Del Mar, was designed and built for the Chart House Restaurant administrative offices, on land originally bought through me by a north county bank, who then sold it when they learned they would not be allowed to erect the drive-through window they had planned.

Joe Lancor's wood and glass building at 853 Camino Del Mar served as corporate offices for Chart House Seafood Restaurants until the company outgrew the office space.

Later, when the Chart House offices required more space, Joe designed the remodel of the Solana Theatre on Acacia Avenue in Solana Beach.

Zel's Del Mar

The building at 1247 Camino Del Mar, was once the local telephone office. When the office relocated in the late 1970s, I was able to sell the building to Zel Camiel, and what a colorful history that building

The restaurant at 1247 Camino Del Mar has changed hands several times since Nancy Hoover first opened her café there, but it has always remained a restaurant.

has had since. Oh, the trauma at City Hall when Nancy Hoover (also the mayor at the time) first leased the building from Zel and turned it into a restaurant — with not enough parking spaces, no place for equipment, and so on. Of course, most people, unaware of the City legal infractions, simply enjoyed the food and conviviality for years. And all the while the owner of the building, Zel, was sitting comfortably enjoying the hullabaloo. Today Zel's Del Mar is owned and operated by Jennifer Powers and Greg Glassman, who is Zel Camiel's grandson.

The Del Mar library

My idea of turning the church-turned-restaurant-turned-commercial-building at 1309 Camino Del Mar into the Del Mar branch of the San Diego County Library stemmed from a visit that my husband, Steve Farrell, and I made to Santa Barbara. It was that special community, with its well-designed buildings and a very nice library, that made me think to myself, "Why doesn't the Del Mar library have its own fine location — instead of being housed in a trailer at the City Hall Annex?" It turned out that the project succeeded because of a combination of timing, other goals of the owners I was representing, the right building and the right people to make it happen.

Our great Del Mar village was filled with interesting people who had gathered here from so many different parts of the world and from such different backgrounds — with varied talents and intellects. So it simply didn't seem right that they and their children had to access books from a former trailer facility in a temporary location in our village.

When my family and I had arrived in Del Mar In the late 1950s, the library was a 9-foot by 12-foot space in a cubby hole on 15th Street beneath a dentist's office, where one now enters the back dining room of Sbicca restaurant. (I did think this was a charming location, but more than restrictive in the space available for books and for parking.) From there the library was moved to Del Mar Plaza, and from there to 14th Street into a space in a new building designed by Don Schoell, local AIA architect, until it was moved again to the annex of the City of Del Mar offices on 11th Street.

It was years later that the transaction for the current library location took place, with the acquisition of the former St. James Catholic Church. The somewhat complicated transition from church to library would begin with some finesse on my part, as I worked to procure that building for my client — an international industrialist seeking headquarters here near his Fairbanks Ranch home. He was intrigued with the idea of having an office with such an interesting history. He was fascinated that the building had originated as a church, and that it housed the Albatross restaurant, which had been established there in 1966 after the church had relocated to Solana Beach. Howard Gad had used a lot of bender board when he and Gordon Denyes changed the use from church to restaurant; it had been rather an extreme makeover of the interior.

Upon inquiring with the owner of the building about whether he might be interested in selling, I was advised, "If you locate another site for my firm's operation, then I will deliver." I went through some trying periods in setting up that transaction. Finally, during the time escrow was open, I moved my own real estate offices into the building for a tad over 30 days in order to establish its use as an office building. Imagine, my desk was in the pulpit!

That was project one. And then a few decades later, owners Ed and Joan Daniel, who had done a massive remodel of the interior to create luxury office space, accepted my idea of selling the building to house the Del Mar branch of the County library. The Del Mar representatives, Councilman Elliot Parks and local businessman Dennis Cruzan, had to complete the transactional agreements and bonding through the City of Del Mar so the escrow could fund and record.

As I'm rereading this, I realize it sounds as if it were easy — all too easy. And no wonder — I left out the part about convincing the

The St. James Catholic Church building was remodeled first as a restaurant and later as luxury offices. It looked like this when Chiquita Abbott Real Estate, Inc. brokered the sale that allowed the property to house the Del Mar branch of the San Diego County Library.

53

County of San Diego that this building could be adapted for operation as a public library. Numerous individuals contributed to the effort, including Pat Freeman, then President of the Friends of the Del Mar Library; Mayor Jacqueline Winterer; and others, without whose influence within the City and the County Library system we would not have our library in its historical site today. The Friends of the Del Mar Library board fought long, and often quietly, to win, and the library opened in its new location in 1996.

Commercial transactions

I have been around long enough to have sold a commercial lot on Camino Del Mar when it was still named Highway 101. The lot was the north half-block between 8th and 9th on the east side of 101, and I was able to sell it twice before it was built upon. No wonder I have a love affair with real estate!

Of course, along with each commercial real estate transfer goes some history. We are sitting on many historical, or mature, sites, and so many times we're not even aware of the history until we get involved in the transaction. What fun it has been to seek out prior ownership records and trace them to the present! Imagine what situations those people ran into as they dealt with the various ordinances in the County of San Diego, the governing body when most of Del Mar's commercial buildings were built.

For me personally, and for brokers in general, a transaction is exhilarating. For it is never without a goal, or a series of goals, creating a terrific incentive. Finding a way to come to the end of a complex commercial transaction with a win-win result is success indeed. And for me, being able to have a long-range result that provides me with a solid business relationship is what it's all about.

Chapter 11

The ocean

I feel compelled to be certain I haven't overlooked sharing some personal experiences and facts about the great love/hate relationship practically everyone around here has with our ocean and how it affects our coastal properties. Truly, when speaking of Del Mar, the impact of the Pacific ocean is at least as enormous as that of the thoroughbred track.

When we love the ocean, we're thinking of basking in the sun, lying on the sandy beach and swimming in the surf — and Del Mar's beaches are second to none.

When we hate it is when — on very rare occasions — heavy winter storms have brought very high and rough tides that left Coast Boulevard flooded at 27th Street, and when the waters simply broke through the windows and walls of our houses.

We have learned to be fearful of these tides when we hear the warning calls. In Del Mar, our local lifeguards have issued such warnings, either as personal telephone calls, or knocks on doors for evacuation and road closings. What a blessing they have been during such times.

We had such storms in 1998 and some of the years that closely followed, storms that inundated the lower floors of the properties adjoining and just north of the L'Auberge hotel. The particular site I refer to now was the four-unit apartment building (it has now been replaced by the stunning white condominium building designed and built by Batter Kay).

The land to the west of the apartment units contained the locally famous concrete sidewalk that some of the early developers had built for easy walking when ladies in their long dresses and hats were escorted by their husbands, who reportedly had each been invited as a prospective buyer of an ocean-front lot. In the 1998 storm, slabs of concrete never before seen by contemporaries became very visible, because the sand that had accumulated over the years had washed away, exposing parts of the buried sidewalk. With subsequent summer seasons after the flooding, the beach was replenished by the natural flow of sand from north to south along the coast and the sidewalk was covered again.

Oh, yes, as managing agents, our role as keepers of those rental units for the owner was to see that waters receded or were pumped away, furniture dried out or was replaced, and frightened tenants were left with calm! That was the period when I learned about "deadmen." Yes, massive concrete blocks installed to give the wooden seawalls some strength by providing support and resisting the waves.

Anyway, it was after that 1998 storm that I became acquainted with Milton (Milt) Smith, husband of Dorothea and dad to local attorney Tricia Smith and her sister, artist Rosemary KimBal. As I was watching Milt and his small crew in that grueling rain, waves breaking over him while he was mending the seawall to bring things back to normal, I reached for able-bodied men to assist, and my poor nephew Alex Meyer swears he still suffers from the heavy, heavy work of that effort.

Chapter 12

Volunteers at the heart of it all

Volunteerism has always been important in the city of Del Mar, and the arrival of UCSD brought with it an army of additional volunteers. The interests of our volunteers run the gamut from the environment to social services, cultural programs to the City budget. All are vital to Del Mar.

Of course, organizing a volunteer effort takes a while, and it takes a lot of learning. But then that kind of effort and caring becomes reflected in an annual invitation from the Mayor and Council members to each active volunteer, to enjoy an evening out at the Powerhouse Community Center, so the City can say thanks in a big way. And one's name is no doubt etched in a big book kept up by our City Managers over the years with the enormous help of City Clerk Mercedes Martin and the many who have followed her.

The Garden Club

The Design Review process described in Chapter 9 eventually became involved not only with building design, but also with landscaping, not just in residential areas, but in commercial zones too. And that presented a problem: Each commercial building needs some sort of buffer. But have you noticed that in Del Mar's commercial areas there's often no room for buffers? The commercial lots are small, and there's simply no place for side-yard planting.

However, in this village we have the Garden Club. And so there are now small planter boxes in front of the downtown shops and other commercial buildings. How many shopkeepers, you may wonder, have the time to water? How many buildings have convenient water outlets? But, of course, the Garden Club schedules members to stop by and see that the plants receive their timely drinks of water — another near miracle made possible by Del Mar's army of talented and willing volunteers.

The median strip

The efforts of volunteers in making our city beautiful are of course complemented by the efforts of the Del Mar City government. A great example is the median strip that runs through the city. Those of us who drive up and down Camino Del Mar daily may or may not have stopped to notice the change in the planting within the median strips. And how many of us remember the huge trees that once graced them?

I am now taking us back to Del Mar's special Council and committees that decided that we did, in fact, need a median strip and that it should contain some plants. The first part to be created would be in the beach area on the north end of town. The active volunteers involved in establishing our median strip solicited the advice and counsel of our most active horticultural expert, Pat Welsh. Our committee consisted of probably a half-dozen people, our own Lou Terrell among them, but we relied on Pat.

To go into the community and ask for funds for an improvement project takes a lot of energy. But in Del Mar every time the need arises, committed people come forward who care enough to put their dollars on the line. For the median-strip project there was one individual in town who started us off with a donation of $10,000. (What a lot of money that was — and he kept his name from us and everyone else.) This seed money did the trick, and we were off to the nursery. We were able to go again and again until the town looked so beautiful.

The City took over the job of watering the plants. Eventually the limbs of the Torrey pines that had been planted in the median (after months of indecision about their use) began to hang over the highway, interfering with visibility. So the pines were removed, the type of landscaping was changed, and the replacement plants were chosen to conserve water.

Just a few more examples

Over the years the Del Mar city government, or simply groups of like-minded citizen volunteers, have established organizations that have become so important to Del Mar life. I'd like to mention just a few of them here, some of the ones I have found so worthwhile.

The **Del Mar Chamber of Commerce** was founded in 1946, and years later I was the first woman to serve on its Board of Directors. This was partly a matter of being in the right place at the right time — I was active in the Del Mar business community (not too many women were) and in volunteer organizations, so the Chamber was a natural fit.

Much more than just a way for Del Mar businesspeople to meet, interact and promote their businesses, the Chamber, from the beginning, served the greater Del Mar community. It supported a Boy Scout Troop; financed street and street-light repairs, street cleaning, tree trimming, and public trash cans; and sponsored many contests and community events.

In 1985 Swede Throneson and others established the **Del Mar Historical Society (DMHS)** as a 501(c)(3) non-profit to discover, record, collect, preserve and display for public benefit historical facts, artifacts, properties and other materials related the the history of Del Mar. This volunteer organization, still active and supported by donations, meets monthly and holds periodic programs for the public.

Volunteer-driven **Del Mar Community Connections (DMCC)** provides programs and services to support Del Mar elders so they can

PHOTO COURTESY OF DEL MAR HISTORICAL SOCIETY

The Alvarado House, the first residence sold in Jacob Taylor's 1885 Del Mar development, was donated to the Del Mar Historical Society, and is currently located on the Del Mar Fairgrounds. The house is open to the public during the San Deigo County Fair, with docents from the Historical Society on site to tell about its history.

continue to thrive in the homes they love. DMCC began when Nancy Weare and her friend Ann Silber recruited the informal network of caring, active Del Martians who were already regularly and quietly reaching out to help others. In 2000 the 501(c)(3) organization was founded, with a volunteer Board of Directors, of which I was one.

DMCC now has two full-time employees and many volunteers. In addition to providing alternative transportation options for older Del Martians, the organization offers a full calendar of educational, cultural and exercise programs and social activities, which provide support, not to mention fun.

The volunteer experience

Del Mar offers many opportunities for individuals and businesses to support special projects and ongoing activities in the community. When we volunteer, we may think we have all the right experience and "know-how." And then we meet someone who has more experience and knows more. Will we be able to contribute enough? If not, it can be a real heartbreaker and an eye opener. I guess if we persist and all goes well, we eventually just drop into the volunteer niches that fit.

Afterword

Seeing through the eyes of Chiquita Abbott over 60-plus years of watching and being a part of Del Mar — what a ride, what a collection of experiences! As a realtor I have been privy to the personal lives of the most creative, yet caring and passionate people living during this period.

As I worked through the process of putting together the manuscript for this book, my intention was not so much to tell you about my life as to tell you a story of Del Mar over the years. But I discovered that the real story of my Del Mar life, the story I most wanted to share, was in the relationships I enjoyed with the strangers I met, and the friendships that developed. I came to the conclusion that readers being able to read about themselves, or others they know, is the real history.

I also learned that writing about what happens is a whole lot faster than living it, and that our memories are not tape recorders. In telling our history, each of us picks out different moments, different highlights, and we may leave some of the details dim. There are, of course, stories of my Del Mar life other than the one told on these pages. Other moments, other strangers met and friendships developed. I, Chiquita Abbott Farrell, have shared here just some of the moments I remember.

If you would like to record other Del Mar moments you remember, I give you permission — no, I encourage you, to write them in the blank spaces in this book — at the ends of some chapters, beyond the index, even on the insides of the covers.

Love,

Chiquita

Index

Made in the USA
Las Vegas, NV
25 November 2022